D0001619

3242

What is your favorite way to eat a banana? How do you know?

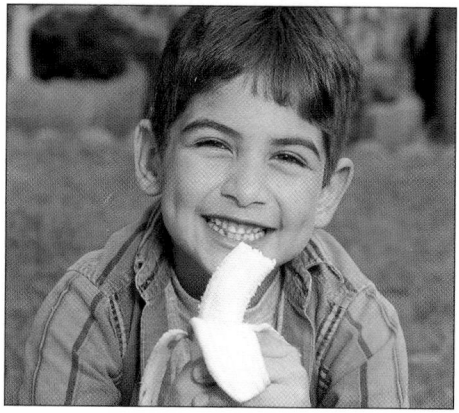

You know because of your sense of taste.

Tasting is one of the five senses. The others are hearing, seeing, touching, and smelling.

The sense of taste begins with your tongue.

Look in the mirror and stick out your tongue.

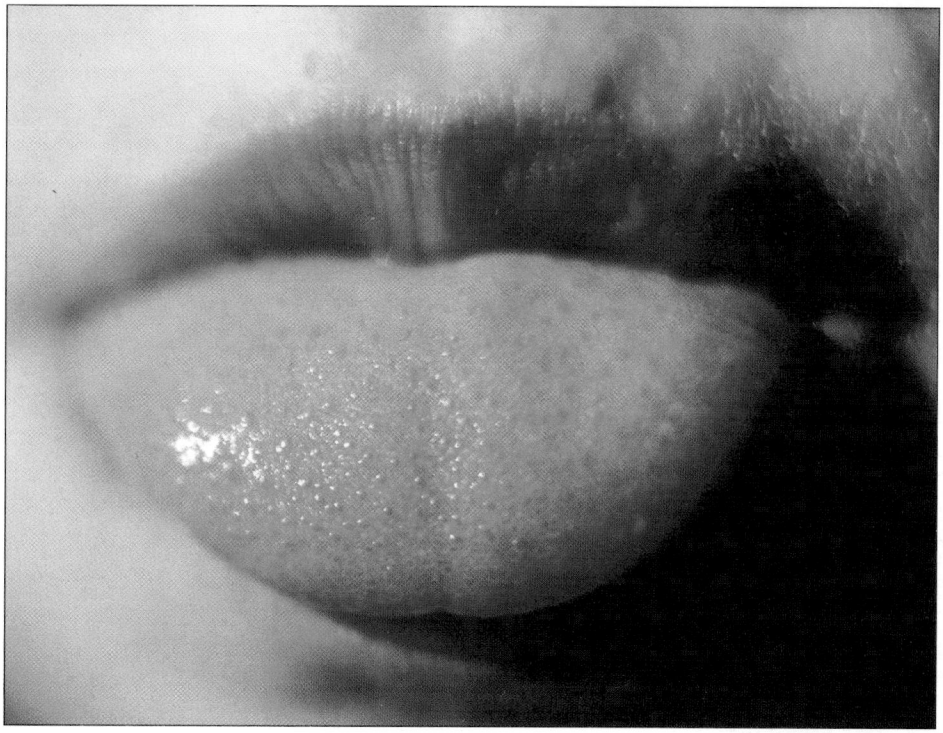

Your tongue is covered with little bumps. Each bump is filled with many taste buds.

The taste buds on the tip of your tongue taste salty and sweet things.

The taste buds on the sides taste sour things.

And the back of your tongue has taste buds for bitter things.

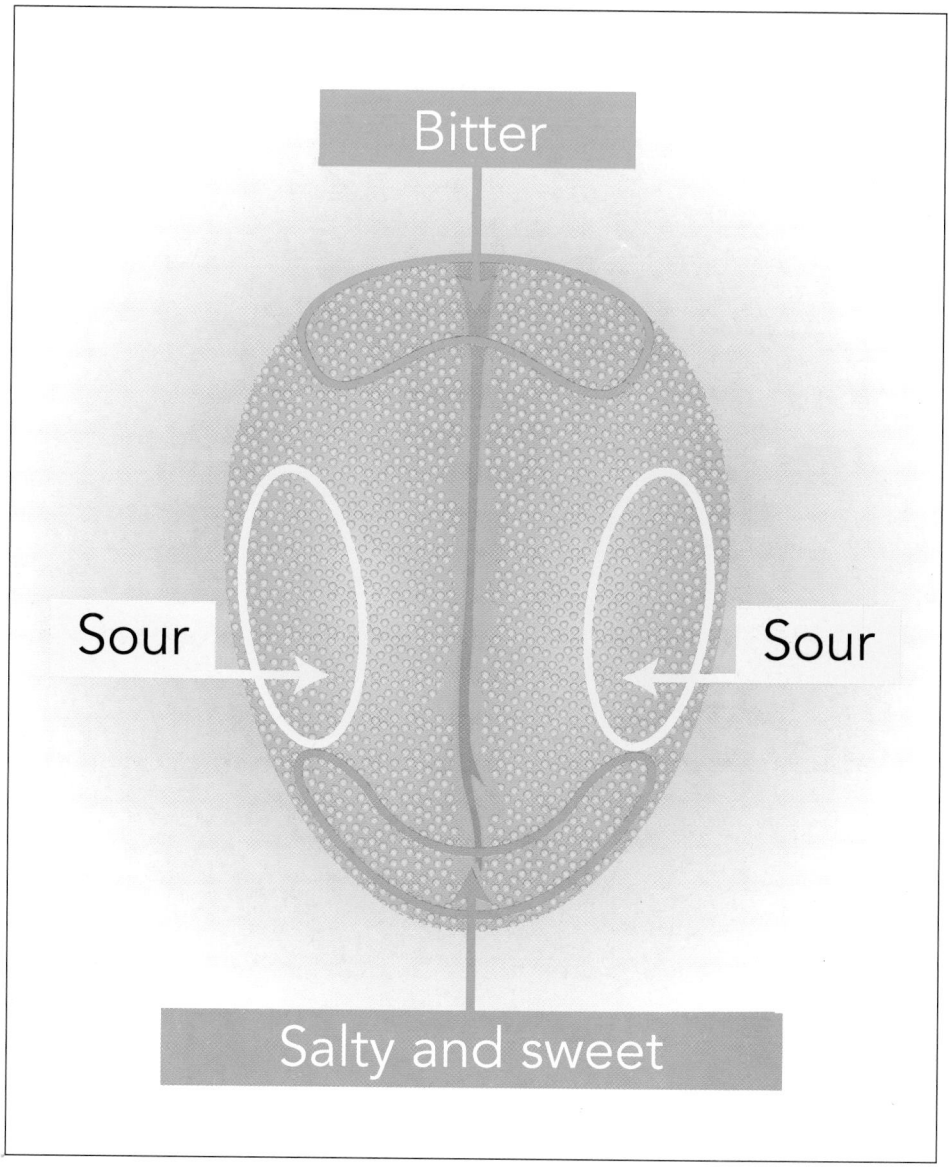
Bitter
Sour
Sour
Salty and sweet

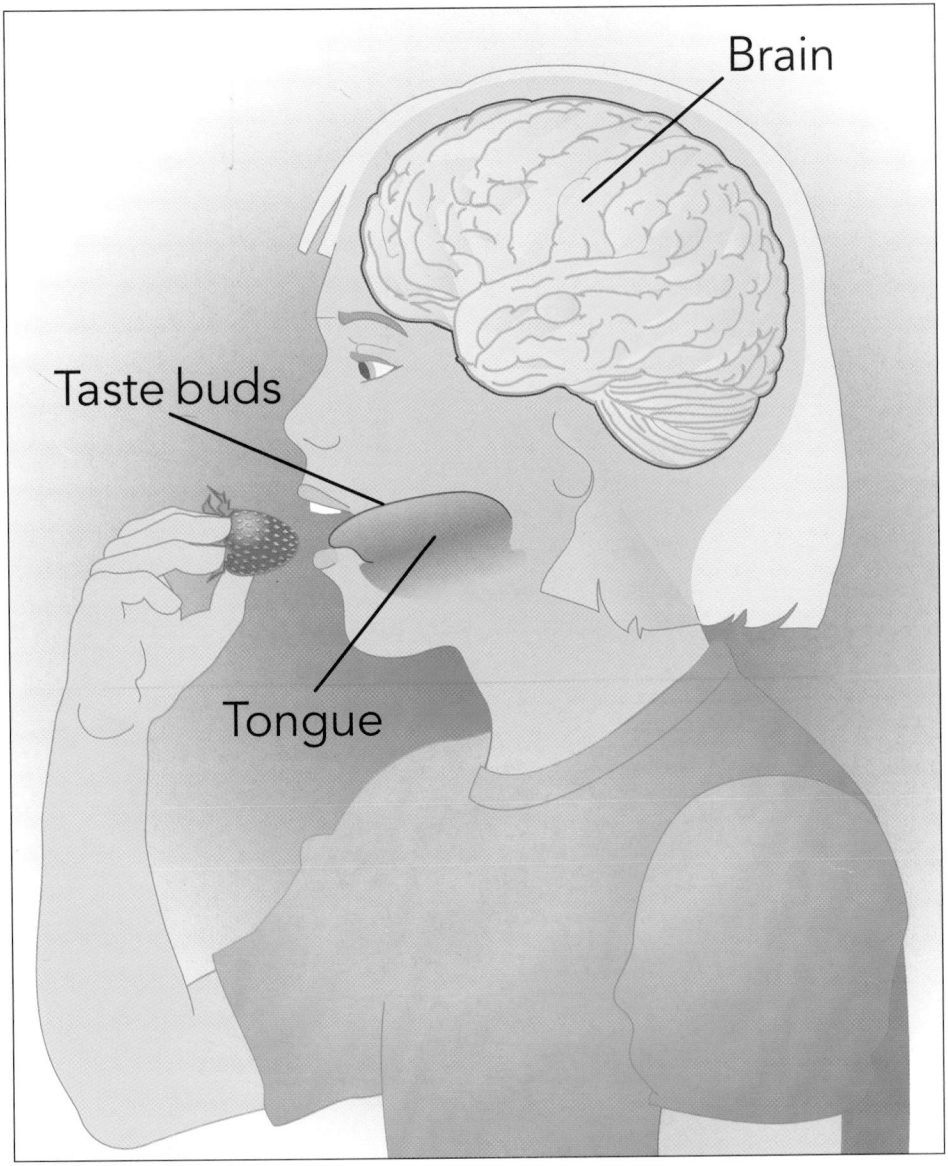
Brain
Taste buds
Tongue

The taste buds tell your brain what you are tasting.

Then your brain tells you if you like what you are eating or drinking.

That is how you taste things.

A picnic is a good place
to try out your taste buds.

You will find lots of good food to taste.

Try the sweet corn.
Do you like it plain or
with some melted butter?

Taste a sour pickle.
What a face!

Look at all the salads. There is something for every taste.

Try some cheese. Each one tastes very different.

This juicy watermelon
looks good to eat.
Watch out for the seeds!

Would you like some of these salty chips?

Many grown-ups like
the taste of bitter coffee.
Do you?

If a lemon is sour, why
is lemonade so sweet?

The secret is lots of sugar!

Do not eat food that has been sitting in the sun too long.

It is always best to throw it away. It could make you sick.

Desserts can be very sweet.

Would you like fresh strawberries or an ice cream cone? Both!

How would you describe the taste of this?

Yummy!

Words You Know

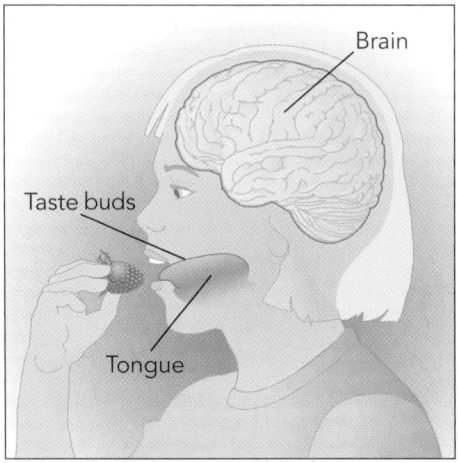

brain

bitter

salty

sour

sweet

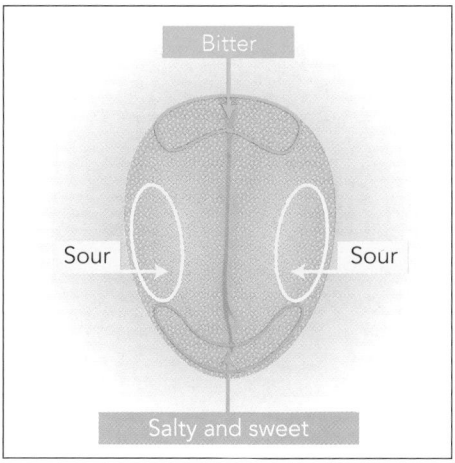

taste buds

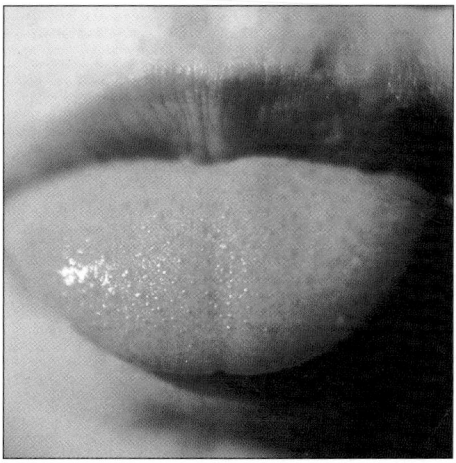

tongue

Index

banana, 3
bitter, 8, 9, 20
brain, 10, 11
butter, 14
cheese, 17
chips, 19
coffee, 20, 21
corn, 14
dessert, 26
five senses, 4
food, 13, 24
ice cream, 27
lemonade, 22, 23
pickle, 15
picnic, 12
salads, 16
salty, 8, 9, 19
sour, 8, 9, 15, 23
strawberries, 26, 27
sugar, 23
sweet, 8, 9, 14, 23, 26
taste buds, 7, 8, 9, 10, 11, 12
tongue, 4, 6, 7, 8, 9, 10
watermelon, 18

About the Author

Sharon Gordon is a writer living in Midland Park, New Jersey. She and her husband have three school-aged children and a spoiled pooch. Together they enjoy visiting the Outer Banks of North Carolina as often as possible.

Photo Credits

Photographs ©: Envision: 16 (Osentoski & Zoda); Nance S. Trueworthy: 15, 17, 19, 25, 30 bottom, 31 top left; Photo Researchers, NY/Dennis Purse: 3 top right; PhotoEdit: 3 bottom left (Mary Kate Denny), 12 (Myrleen Ferguson Cate), cover (Felicia Martinez), 3 top left, 3 bottom right, 22 (Michael Newman), 26 (Robin L. Sachs), 27, 31 top right (D. Young-Wolff); Rigoberto Quinteros: 5, 6; Stock Boston: 24 (Bill Bachmann), 13 (Steven Frame), 28 (Jean-Claude Lejeune); Stone: 14 (Sara Gray), 7, 31 bottom right (Roy Gumpel);Viesti Collection, Inc.: 21, 30 top right (M.G. Perelli/Ask Images), 18 (Robert Winslow).

Illustrations by Patricia Rasch.